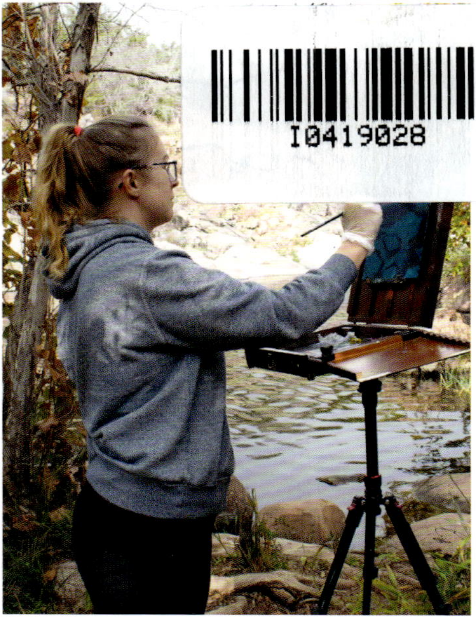

02 ART SUPPLIES AND EQUIPMENT

In order to make plein air painting a regular practice, it is important to make it accessible. I find the best way to achieve this is to have a dedicated plein air pack that I can grab and go. In fact, I have a few of these that are tailored to either oil painting or water-based media. They range from extremely simple kits that I can throw into a tote bag or fanny pack, to small bins loaded with everything I might want for a full day dedicated to painting on location.

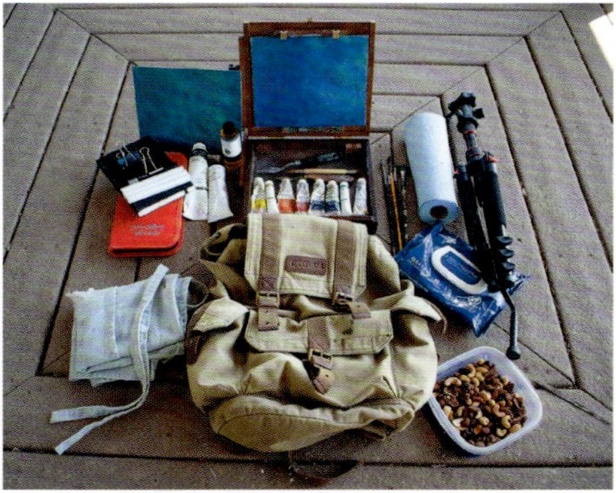

- **Backpack** or other carrying mechanism: Consider your individual preferences for how much you are comfortable carrying when deciding on the type of bag, then make decisions regarding your art supplies based on that.
- **Checklist** of everything you need: This makes it easy for you to quickly gather some essential supplies.
- **Viewfinder:** This can just be a piece of cardboard with a properly proportioned rectangle/square cut out of it, a small plastic device with a slide that adjusts the proportions of the windows, or just an approximation that you make with your thumbs and index fingers.
- **Sturdy rigid backing:** No matter your medium, you will likely need some kind of rigid support for your painting substrate. If you are painting on paper, you may want to just bring a drawing board to attach your paper to, or a watercolor block. With watercolor and gouache, I find it easy to use a sketchbook with a metal palette magnetized to one side of the spread while I paint on the other side. A brush with a water reservoir eliminates the need to have a cup of water. I can hold this kit with my non-dominant hand and paint anywhere without having to unpack a bag and set up any equipment. If you are painting with oils or acrylics, you may want an easel or pochade box to hold your panel or stretched canvas. For substrates mounted to a hard

backing (like canvas panels), I have found that I can simply use bulldog clips to attach them directly to my mixing palette (pictured below). For me, this is a great minimalist set up that doesn't bog me down with the weight of an easel or pochade box. There are also small, lightweight pochade boxes that can be held in your non-dominant hand (see 23 for an example).

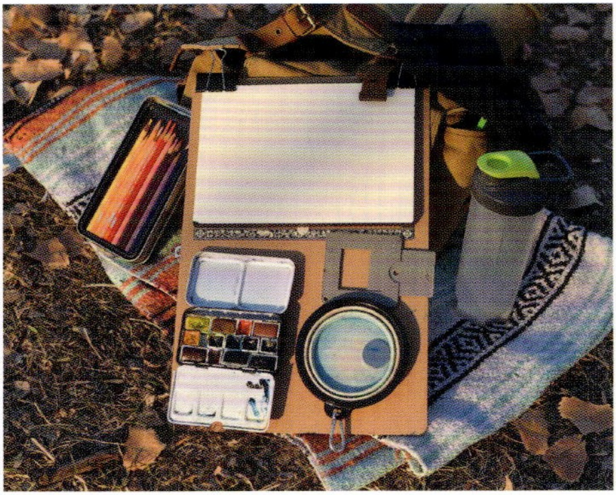

- **Sketching material:** You can use a sketchbook or scratch paper for sketching. I like the small Field Notes notebooks that are 5.5×3.5 inches. I like having two or three shades of gray markers to do quick value-based compositions, a 4-color ballpoint pen (you can layer the colors to get a surprising range of color out of these, and hatching will get you a full range of values), and graphite or charcoal.

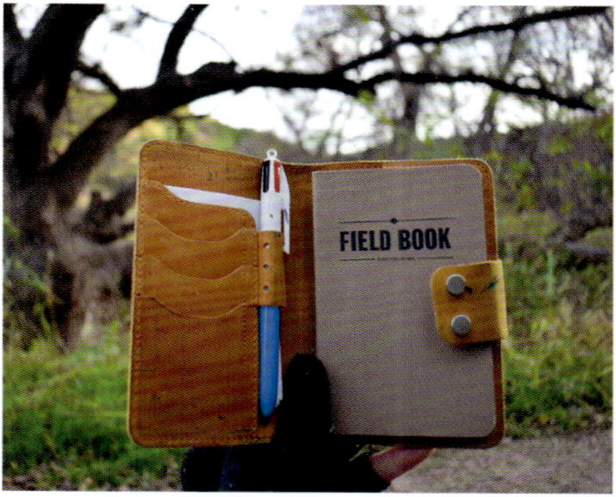

ITEMS FOR COMFORT

- **Clothing:** You should wear clothing that is comfortable and appropriate for the weather, but you should also choose your clothing according to how it might impact your color perception. You may not consider the color of your clothing to be part of the painting process, but on a sunny day the sun can cause the color of your garments to reflect upon your substrate and impact the way you see the colors you're mixing. Most important are the colors you wear on or around your face and your upper body. Clothing on the lower half of your body is less likely to be reflected onto your painting. Use sunscreen on any exposed skin.

- **White umbrella:** Having an umbrella is usually not necessary, but it can certainly make painting more comfortable. In the windswept prairie where I spend most of my time painting, an umbrella is not often worth the trouble of fighting the wind gusts. But an umbrella can provide shade to you and your painting set up that will protect your skin and eyes from the sun while also making it easier for you to judge color on your palette.
- **Hat (neutral color):** If you are wearing a hat with a brim, try to choose a hat in a light neutral color. If you feel the need to wear sunglasses, understand that this may impact how you see the colors and values in what you observe and in how you mix your paint.
- **Insect protection:** Bug repellent, mosquito nets (there are some that cover your head), bug repellant candles or devices.
- **A note about linseed oil and bugs:** If you are painting with oils, be aware that most oil paints are made with linseed

oil and other organic oils that actually attract many insects. In addition to pestering you, insects will be drawn directly to your paints and painting. It can be frustrating to see little insects diving into your beautiful painting, and you may find yourself trying to dig them out with your palette knife. I am here to tell you that your efforts will be in vain and you should give up. You will spend more time fighting these pests than actually painting. So let them be. You will be able to remove them once you're back home and your painting is still wet. Frankly, at this point I consider most insects and other natural elements that find their way into my paintings as a beautiful contribution from Mother Nature.

BATHROOM NEEDS

Some of us need to consider bathroom needs before going out to paint. If I'm going to be out painting for more than just a couple of hours, I need to know how I can address these needs. I have found myself in the unfortunate position of being in the middle of a plein air painting session and suddenly needing to use a restroom. Because there were no restrooms at the park where I had set up, and because it is a public park with many visitors, I had to just pack up and go home. Now, if I want to paint somewhere with no restrooms, I know it's likely going to be a short session.

- **Plan your location:** You don't need to pick out the exact spot from where you will paint, but you will know generally where you're going for the day. If you are unfamiliar with a location, do some research ahead of time to find out what amenities are available to you.
- **Portable urinals/wet wipes:** If your location is sufficiently secluded you may consider making it comfortable and sanitary to "go" on location. There are portable urinals tailored for female needs that make it possible to eliminate outdoors with some level of privacy and cleanliness. Do a search online for "female urinal" and you will find many options. If you decide to use wet wipes or toilet paper outdoors, please be sure not to litter these items. Bring a bag for waste and dispose of it properly in designated receptacles. I reiterate, this option is *not* for everyone, but for those who are comfortable with it, it's an option as long as you are responsible and not at risk for exposing yourself to others. Wear clothing conducive to this need, such as a dress or skirt or pants with an elastic waist.

FOOD AND WATER

- **Drinking water:** Plan to bring an appropriate amount of drinking water to ensure you stay hydrated.

- **Coffee/tea in a thermos**
- **Snacks:** Bring food that requires no refrigeration or heating and that keeps well. Suggestions: Trail mix, nuts, seeds, legumes, jerky/dehydrated protein, and dehydrated fruit. (I love dehydrated mango! It's a special treat I reserve for plein air ventures.)

Note: Be mindful of your hands—Even if you're using non-toxic paint, make sure your hands are clean before using them to eat.

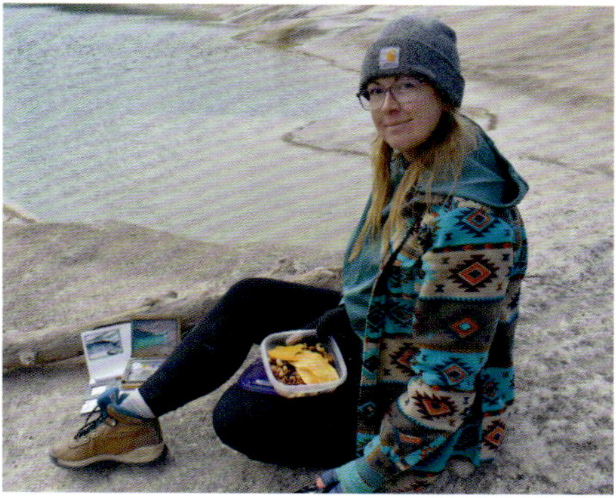

Taking a break with my favorite plein air snack of dried mangos.

SITTING VS. STANDING

Something you may not have considered is whether you are more comfortable sitting or standing. Most of the time, plein air set ups accommodate artists who like to stand. Easels and pochade boxes mounted to tripods can be adjusted to suit standers or those who would rather sit in a chair. If you like sitting in a chair, consider bringing your own lightweight chair. In my case, I actually prefer sitting on the ground, so I'll bring just a blanket to sit on.

- **Chair:** This will likely be the most comfortable option if you like to paint while sitting. There are "ultralight" chairs made for backpackers that weigh just a pound or two and they can be extremely comfortable.
- **Blanket/outdoor cushion:** Lately for me just a blanket on the ground is usually enough to be comfortable for up to an hour. Any longer than that and my posture suffers, and my legs fall asleep.
- **Picnic table/park bench:** In many locations, you'll have access to benches or tables. These are usually strategically placed in nice spots, and you may be able to move tables to some limited extent. But overall, this may prove to be a comfortable option with limited flexibility.
- **Tree stump/large rock:** Look for natural structures that are comfortable and safe to sit on.

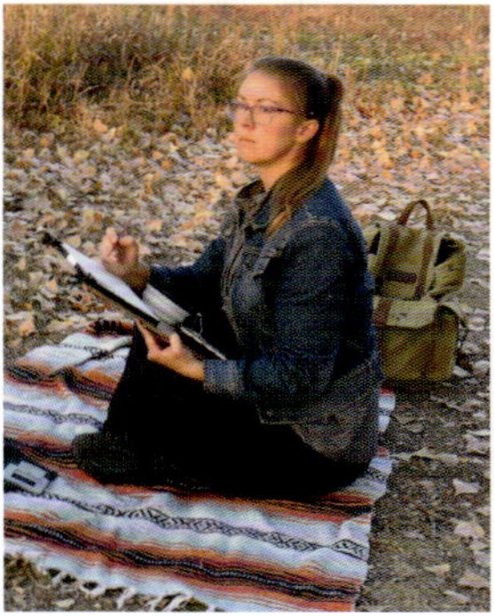

I don't mind sitting on the ground sometimes.

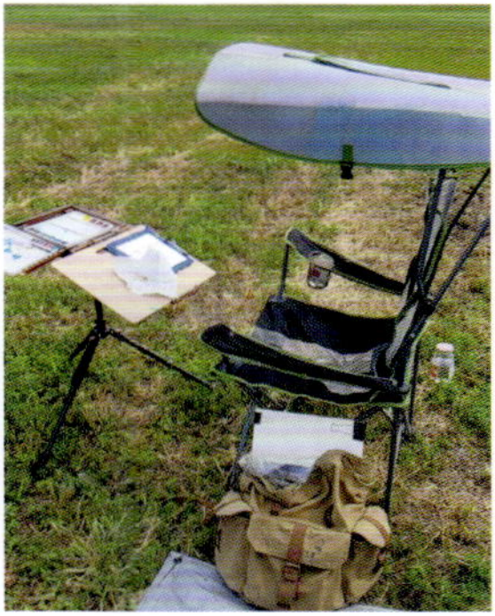

I'll bring my folding chair if I don't have to carry it far.

03 SKETCHING

I must admit that I am guilty of not always sketching prior to beginning a painting. When I do sketch, however, I never regret it, and I firmly believe it always makes my painting better. Sketching is a bit like warming up before a workout. You can get by and still have a productive session without it, but you'll notice that sessions where you do your warm-up are consistently better.

Sketching allows you to begin the visual problem-solving process. When painting, you may encounter elements that didn't initially strike you as particularly challenging, but now that you're painting, you're not sure how to proceed and you end up doing a lot of fiddling in an area that isn't even your focal point. Doing small, simplified sketches ahead of time will draw your attention to these challenges sooner. With the blunt tools (like a few markers or a stick of charcoal) you're using to sketch, you will be forced to think about how to simplify complexities in the environment.

I recommend having just a small, cheap sketchbook, lined notebook, or even just scratch paper (if you find sketchbooks a bit intimidating or precious) and very limited sketching utensils. The media you choose to use for sketching is completely up to you. I tend to switch between gray markers and ballpoint pens, myself. I have sketchbooks full of "ugly" sketches that I take to the field with me, and I do not feel pressured to have visually appealing sketches because I simply never show these to anyone. I also use paperclips to mark off the next available page in my sketchbook, so I do not flip through it very often to see sketches that I don't like, as I find it discouraging.

PAPER AND MARKER/PENCIL: TRULY, THIS IS ALL YOU NEED!

Notan and Value Thumbnails

This type of sketch should contain two values (black and white), up to a maximum of four values (black, white, and one or two shades of gray). Strictly speaking, a notan is just black and white and forces you to mass elements by making them black or leaving them the white of the paper. For this type of sketch, you need just your paper and one utensil like a black marker, stick of charcoal, pencil, or ink pen.

My own approach to notan sketching is a bit different. I typically begin with a mid-value and white. I find that identifying the mid and light values first works well both for opaque media like oils and gouache, as well as transparent media like watercolor. Once I've identified the large mid-value elements, leaving white only for light values and highlights, I then go to my darkest (black) value to add structure over the mid values. If highlights are particularly prominent and important, I will use an additional light value (a light gray marker, or lighter hatching with my pen or pencil) to denote lights from the highlights that remain the white of the paper. If working on a toned paper, you may want a white charcoal or a white gel pen to add highlights and use the toned paper for your mid values.

When sketching, make note of the way light hits your subject and the relationship of values. You may need to make a deliberate effort to disregard color at this stage. For most of us, sketching should focus on the composition of the elements and the relationships between values.

I try to spend no more than 10 minutes sketching. Sometimes I'll find that a single sketch is sufficient because I am already pretty set on my composition. But it's more common for me to do up to three small "thumbnail" sketches that allow me to compare a few different composition ideas. There are no details in my sketches, and they are often messy, but they do the job of getting me into painting mode.

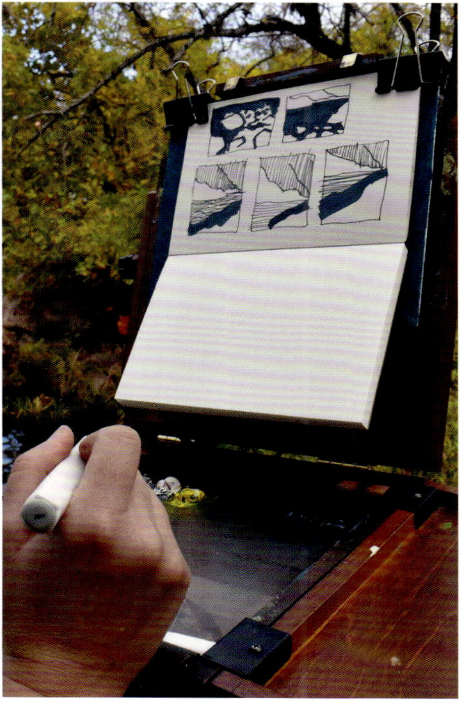

04 OIL PAINTING PLEIN AIR MATERIALS

OIL PAINTING SETUP

- ☑ Painting support of choice (easel, pochade, or a palette with clips)
- ☑ Pre-toned panels (bring at least a couple more than you plan to use)
- ☑ 4 or 5 colors in small tubes
- ☑ Small amount of your medium of choice (optional)
- ☑ 1 brush (a maximum of 3) and/or a palette knife
- ☑ Paper towels
- ☑ Latex gloves
- ☑ Bag for waste
- ☑ Comfort items like beverages, snacks, apron, gloves, hat, etc.

EASEL? POCHADE? NONE OF THE ABOVE?

We addressed this previously, but here I will go into a bit more detail about the factors that you should weigh when deciding how you will prop up your painting surface.

Easel: A simple tripod easel can be easy to fold up and also lightweight. You can find them to be inexpensive and versatile in terms of the size of substrate they will hold. Often, there is no place to set a mixing palette so you may need to hold your palette in your non-dominant hand. Some tripod easels are still very long even when folded up, so it may not fit inside a bag.

French easel: In my mind, the French easel is the quintessential symbol of plein air painting. It is aesthetically pleasing when set up and has great utility. Whether it is a full or half French easel, there is a drawer that can hold tubes of paint and brushes. Once you learn to set it up, it is surprisingly easy and fast. The "half" French easel refers not to the weight, but just the width of the easel. It is actually not much lighter than the full version, but it's easier to fit into a bag and it still accommodates a wide array of canvas or panel sizes. I use my French easel when I do not need to carry it far and when I want to put on a bit of a show for passers-by. This easel draws attention and has a classic look. However, it is heavy and difficult to carry, especially when loaded up with supplies. I would not take this device with me on a hike, though I love the idea of setting up a big beautiful French easel on the peak of a mountain! Maybe one day when I'm rich and famous, I will have one air-dropped to the top of a mountain by helicopter!

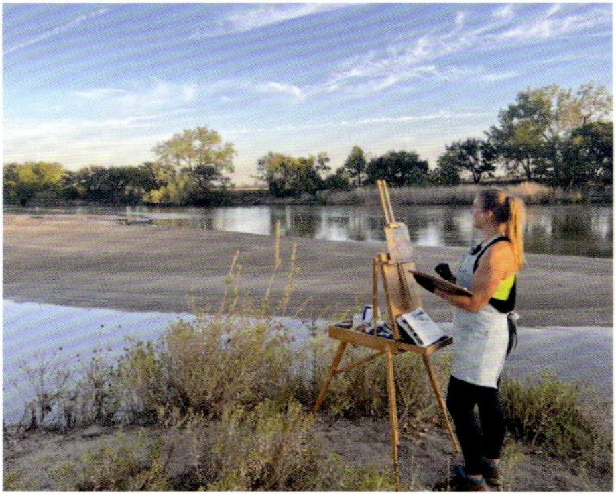

Pochade box: Pochade boxes are becoming increasingly popular among plein air painters. This is a box that is meant to be a self-contained painting support and palette. There are many options out there and you will find mass-produced boxes as well as artist-produced boxes with a wide array of features, complexities, and sizes. Some pochade boxes include storage for paint tubes and brushes, while others are extremely low-profile and easy to pack. Most pochade boxes include an attachment on the bottom that enables them to be mounted to a photography tripod. But some pochade boxes are small, lightweight and are meant to be held in one hand. Pochade boxes tend to be more expensive than other options.

I would recommend getting some painting experience under your belt with less expensive supports and then begin to make note of your preferences.

Pochade box with a tripod: The benefits of a pochade that can be mounted to a tripod are many. You can manage a larger, more complex box with storage and attachments. If you prefer to stand, the tripod's telescoping legs allow you to adjust to the height that works best for you, and you can also adjust it to a sitting height, of course. With the tripod-mounted pochade, the only time you need to consider the weight of the pochade box is when you are carrying it to and from your plein air location. While painting, the tripod supports the weight of the box. You will need to be sure to get a tripod of good quality. There are cheap tripods out there that will eventually fail you, and the last thing you want is for your painting and potentially expensive box to crash to the ground. The drawbacks of this type of box are that it can be somewhat heavy, depending on how it's outfitted. Some pochades contain a glass mixing palette, which is a nice paint surface, but it also adds weight. The material the box is made out of can be heavy, and boxes that are not low-profile will take up a lot of space in a bag or backpack. Additionally, a good quality tripod can cost nearly as much as the box it supports. If you don't want to become the center of attention while out painting in public, a pochade is less attention grabbing than a French easel, but it is certainly not stealthy.

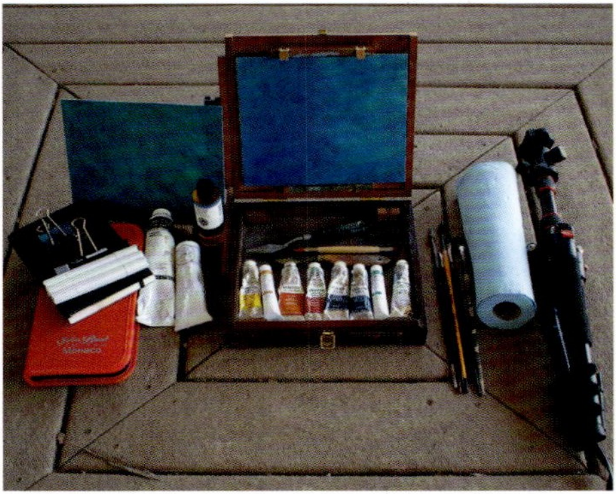

Handheld pochade box: While less common, a handheld pochade box is a great option. It is intentionally low-profile and lightweight because it is meant to be held in your non-dominant hand while you paint. Some have a thumb hole (much like a traditional handheld painting palette) or can be otherwise held comfortably in one hand. It accommodates a small canvas panel and has a small mixing palette. You can stand or sit with it comfortably and it is easy to pack. It is also quite inconspicuous, so if you want to paint without drawing the attention of others, this is a good way to go. A pochade that is small and light enough to be held in one hand will obviously not have the bells and whistles you might find on a more traditional pochade box. It will be more limited in terms of the size of panel it will hold, it will not likely be able to store any of your paints or brushes, and the mixing area will be smaller. Because I can often complete more than one small painting when I go out, I find that I need a way to carry wet oil paintings. We'll address this need further in "Transporting Wet Paintings" in this section.

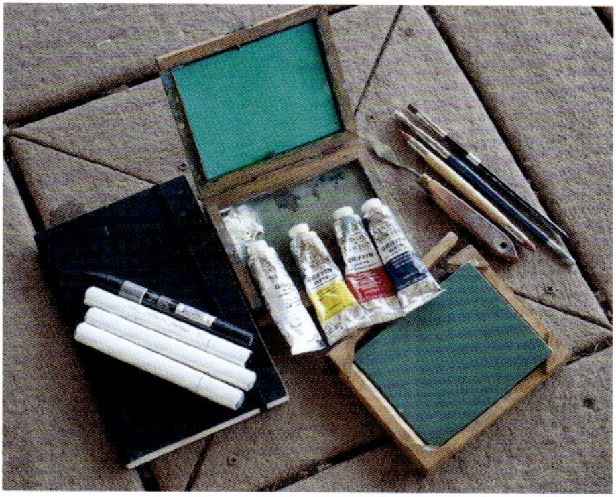

Mixing palette with clips: The simplest, cheapest, most compact way to plein air paint with oil paints is simply to clip a panel to the top portion of a rectangular mixing palette. This is the lowest barrier to entry for plein air painting with oils and I highly recommend trying this if you haven't yet purchased an easel or box. This allows you to try plein air painting without a significant financial investment and you still get the full experience. Be mindful that it is very likely that the palette and paint will come into contact with your clothing, so wear an apron or clothing you don't need to keep pristine. When I paint with this setup, I prefer to mix and apply paint with just a palette knife. It's the most minimal oil painting setup that I've come up with so far, and it makes the process very accessible and enjoyable.

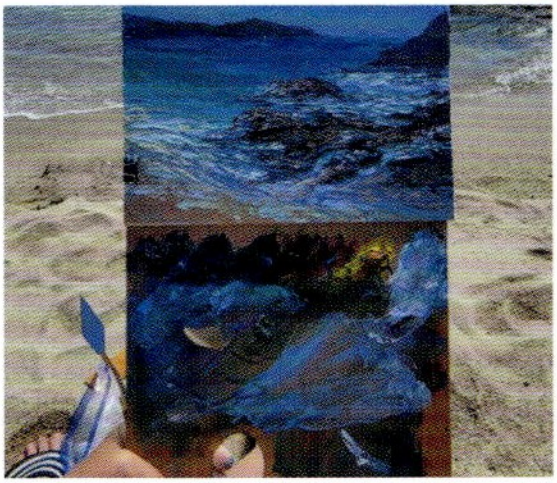

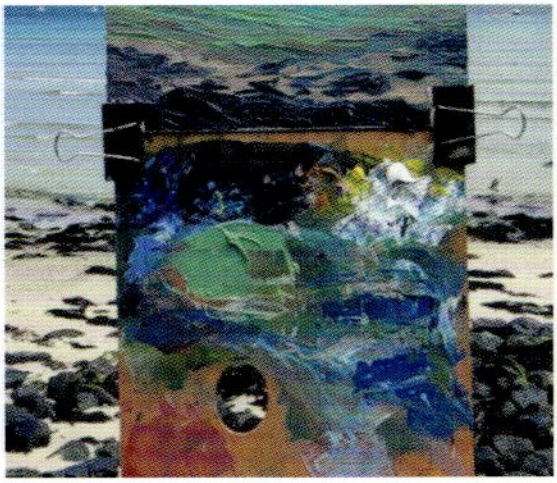

When I went to England, I didn't want to pack anything heavy, so I just clipped my painting panel directly to my palette and painted in oils with just a palette knife.

PAINT AND MEDIUMS

Even if you use a more robust array of pigments in your studio, I suggest using a very limited palette for plein air painting. It will force you to develop a nuanced sense of color relations, and it will also be easier to tote around fewer tubes of paint.

I am not one to suggest specific colors, and I frequently experiment with different limited palettes. There is no "right" or "wrong" about it, and there is no such thing as a pigment that represents a "true" primary yellow, blue, or red. Worry less about the particular pigments, and just try to limit yourself to a yellow, a blue, a red, and a white. Sometimes I like to add just one "dazzling" color to my limited palette. Recently, I used a color called "Amethyst" in addition to my primary palette and used it in nearly all of my mixes. Sometimes I'll replace a more typical yellow, blue, or red with something a bit different—such as Turquoise for my blue, Raw Sienna for my yellow, or Quinacridone Magenta for my red. You can mix, match, and experiment all you want, but try to have no more than four colors plus white on your plein air palette at any given time. You'll find that the secondaries you are able to create are greatly impacted by your pigment selection. This is a great way to introduce yourself to the properties of new pigments without "losing" them in a palette with many colors available to choose from.

The one specific recommendation I'll make regarding pigments is to avoid pigments made from cadmiums, cobalts, and lead. It's not that I never use these pigments (I do use them in studio) and it's not that they aren't great. But when painting outdoors, I am especially mindful of not inadvertently contaminating nature. Though I pack out all of my waste, you never know if a gust of wind will take away your paper towel covered in paint. Or that your palette won't get knocked to the ground. Better safe than sorry, in my opinion, and I just don't use toxic pigments out in nature. Plus, when I'm deeply focused on painting and trying to paint quickly, I'm more likely to make mistakes that result in getting paint on my hands and face. Most pigments available are not toxic. Most of the toxic pigments also happen to be very expensive and come with some indication that they are toxic, so it's not likely you'll accidentally end up with toxic pigments on your palette without you knowing.

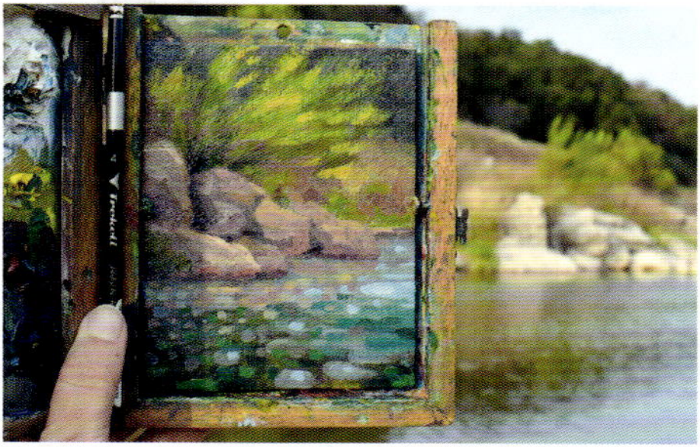

For this painting, I used a traditional primary palette which consisted of Titanium White, Winsor Yellow, Permanent Alizarin Crimson, and Prussian Blue.

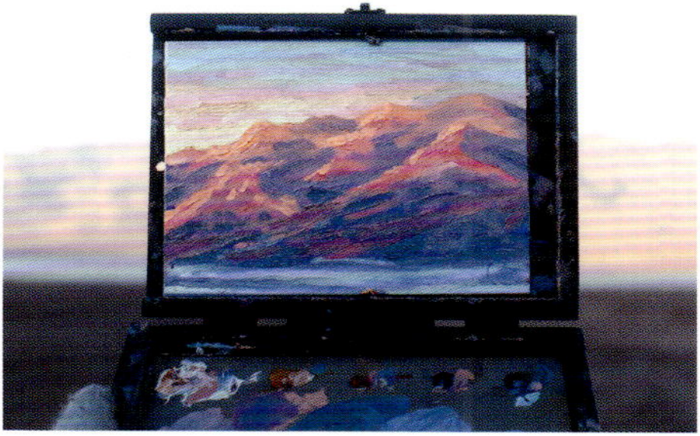

Here you can see that I used a limited palette but with some less-traditional colors. I used Titanium White, Indian Yellow, Indian Red, Amethyst, and Indigo.

Quality of Paint

Using a limited palette has the added benefit of enabling you to purchase a few small tubes of high-quality paint. Just as I do not recommend specific pigments, I am one who doesn't have much brand preference for paints. I recommend purchasing the best-quality paints you can, regardless of brand. Yes, some brands offer paint that is more or less pasty or oily, but you will learn to love whatever you use the most. Be aware that many well-known brands have more than one line of paint. For example, Winsor & Newton has their Winton line of oil paints that are more entry level than their artists' paints, but they are still good quality. Many brands offer paints in a set. If you purchase a set with many pigments, try to pick out just three or four colors plus white to use at a time.

Brush Cleaning with Linseed Oil or Solvents

Most oil paints are made with linseed oil, but I'm referring to having a bottle of linseed oil to use both as a medium and a cleaning agent. I personally almost never add linseed oil to my paints (more on mediums shortly), so the main function of linseed oil for me is actually to clean my brush. Solvents are largely used for brush cleaning (and in some aspects of the painting process itself), but this is actually unnecessary. Furthermore, solvents are a greater risk to your health and the environment than toxic pigments. Solvents create fumes in the air and should never come into contact with the ground. There is no solvent that is completely safe, as they all create fumes. Odorless mineral spirits are toxic just like turpentine. I've used alternate solvents made from citrus oils and lavender, and they smell much better than other solvents, but they are still toxic and also quite expensive. To clean my brushes, I dip them in linseed oil and wipe them off in a paper towel. I just no longer use solvent in the early stages of painting.

The other option is just to bring nothing to clean your brushes other than some good quality paper towels. You can use the towels to wipe off excess paint build up from your bristles, but then just be diligent about cleaning your brushes further when you get home where you can use linseed oil or solvent in a more controlled environment.

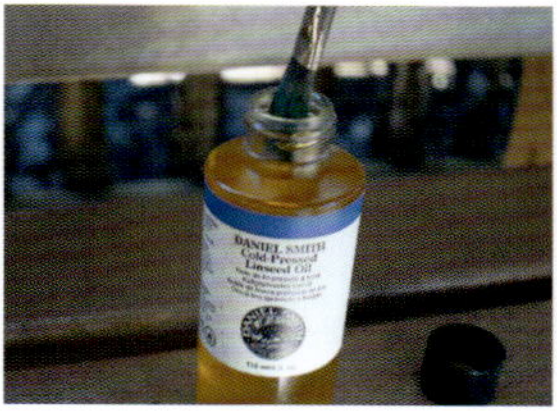

After wiping the excess paint off in a paper towel, I dip my brush in linseed oil.

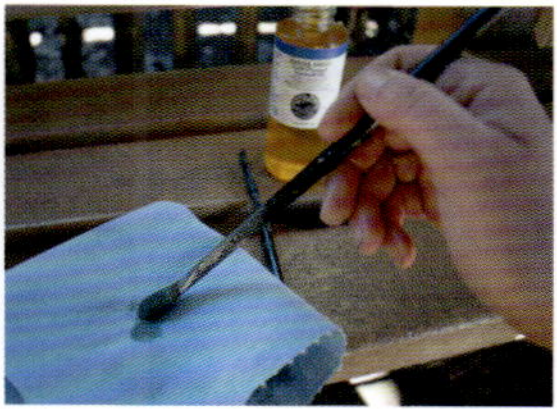
Next, I use the paper towel to remove the oil and as much paint as possible.

Mediums

Painting mediums are meant to impact the flow, viscosity, sheen, dry time, and other properties of your paint. There are many mediums available to you with different properties, but like anything else in plein air painting, I recommend keeping it simple. Linseed oil is the most common painting medium, and you can increase the fluidity of your paint by adding just a little. It is not toxic and can be very affordable. I personally only use Liquin Impasto medium when I plein air paint. It is made by Winsor & Newton, but you can find other brands of alkyd mediums, as well. The main benefit of an alkyd medium is that it makes your paint cure (or dry) much more quickly than it would on its own or with additional linseed oil added. You need to add just a small amount to your mixes to get this quick-dry feature. And when I say "quick," I do not mean that your paint will set up that day. It will still take at least three days, but that is in comparison to a week or two with other mediums or no mediums added.

There now are some brands that make paints with an alkyd medium pre-mixed in. These are a good option for plein air painting. But I find that I like using a white with an alkyd pre-mixed, and because so many of my plein air mixes contain white, I don't really need the other colors to contain alkyd on their own. Some pigments also dry quicker on their own than others. For example, Raw Umber and Ultramarine Blue tend to dry quickly, while Titanium White and most yellows dry more slowly.

Like brush cleaning materials, painting mediums are completely optional. If I didn't use Liquin to help my paintings dry faster, I wouldn't use any medium for plein air painting. When I'm in the field, I'm not as concerned with the viscosity or flow of my paints because I'm doing a quick alla prima (wet-on-wet) sketch that needs no complication.

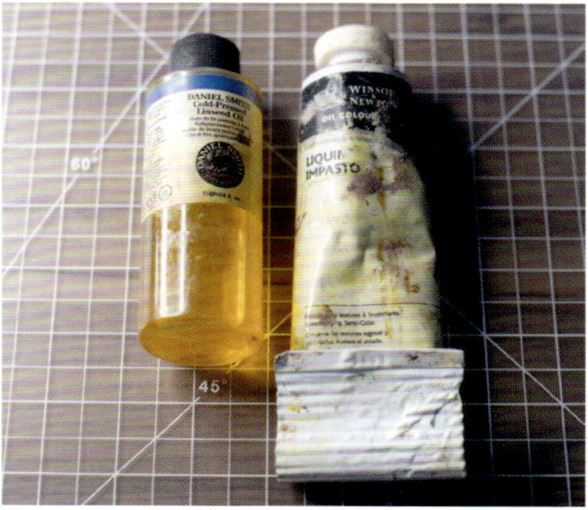

The only mediums I have are linseed oil and Liquin. Mediums are not required and are completely dependent on your preferences.

Disposing of Extra Paint or Solvents

It is important to be mindful of how you will dispose of waste. Since I use non-toxic pigments, I can use a paper towel to remove paint from my brushes and palette, and then either throw these away in designated waste receptacles on-site or put them in a plastic bag and take them home to dispose of them. Never dump solvents on the ground or pour them into water. We should aim to maintain or improve the health of the environments in which we paint. If you do use toxic pigments and solvents, research proper disposal sites in your area and always pack these out after a plein air painting session.

SUBSTRATES

Panels

Canvas or linen adhered to a rigid surface like wood or cardboard is what is commonly referred to as a "panel," but it can be any material that is rigid and low-profile. You can purchase these pre-made in bulk packs or you can make your own. Canvas panels are less expensive than linen panels. Oil-primed panels will cost more than gesso or acrylic primed panels. I prefer the mental freedom of using less expensive panels. If you make your own, be sure to use an acid-free rigid support, acid-free adhesive, and prime your substrate with oil primer or gesso to prevent the oils of your paints from sinking into the substrate.

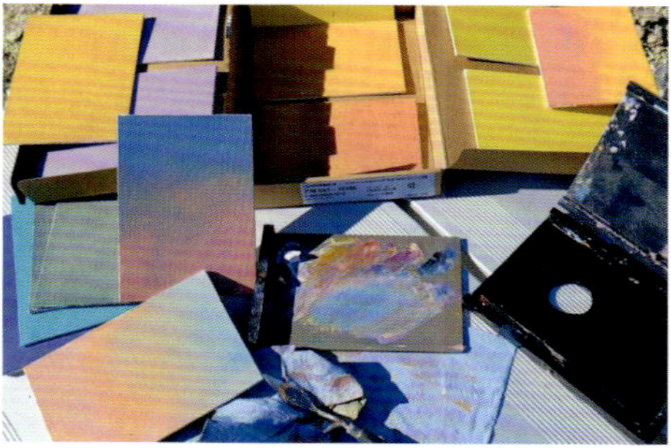

When I have paint left over from a session, I like to use it to tone more panels. Usually, I mix in an alkyd medium like Liquin to help these panels dry faster.

Consider Painting Small

You are free to plein air paint as small or large as you prefer. The most important factor is your level of comfort with a given size. To you, an 8×10-inch panel may feel very small because you're used to painting 18×24-inch or similar sizes. To me, an 8×10 is just about the largest size I want to paint outdoors. I often paint smaller, such as 5×7, 8×8, 4×5, or even 4×4 inches, because these smaller sizes enable me to paint more quickly and also force me to simplify. But my 4×4 might be your 16×16. So, paint a size within your comfort zone, but err on the side of painting smaller rather than whatever you consider to be a regular size when you're studio painting and have the luxury of time and comfort.

Stretched Canvas

Canvas or linen stretched over a stretcher-bar frame is what most people envision for oil or acrylic paintings. They look nice and are at least somewhat lightweight. You have a choice between canvas or linen, and between oil primer or gesso/acrylic primer. Additionally, you can purchase or make stretched canvases with various profile widths—from as low-profile as a half inch, to high profiles like 2 or 3 inches of depth on the sides. Stretched canvases are a little trickier to transport when wet. Another drawback is that stretched fabric can change in tautness over time and may need to be re-stretched from time to time.

Paper

It is possible to oil paint or acrylic paint on paper. Search for oil paper or canvas paper and you'll find papers primed specifically for oil painting, or papers that can be used for either oil or acrylic. These papers are usually thick, at least 100-pound papers. You can use clips to attach paper to a rigid backing or you can use acid-free glue if you want to permanently mount paper to a board. Paper is lightweight and easier to store, but it would require mounting to be made suitable for framing.

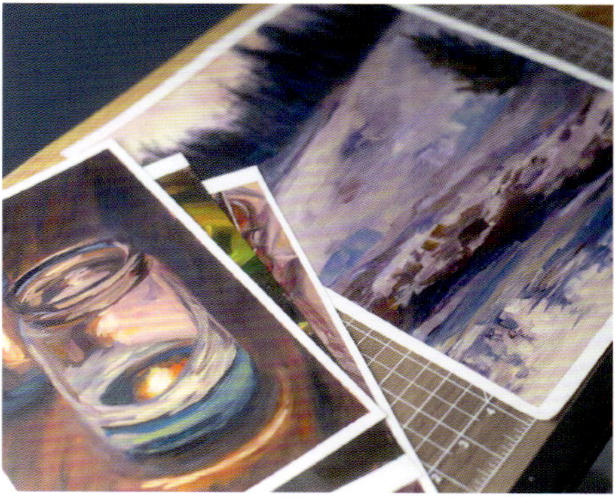

A few examples of oil paintings on paper. You can simply tape or clip the paper to a rigid backing.

Board

One of the most affordable substrates for oil painting is hardboard (a compressed wood surface); you can even use cardboard. Both require priming to prevent oil from absorbing into the substrate. This absorption looks bad, and it also will cause the substrate to rot and decompose. But with proper priming, this is a very affordable and customizable way to paint. I've never used cardboard myself, but obviously it would be easy to cut a lot of it down to any dimensions you'd like, and it's basically free if you re-use packaging.

Hardware stores will often have remnants of hardboard sheets, but even a full 4×8-foot sheet is usually under $30. The hardware store in my area will actually cut a sheet down to small boards of any size I choose. From a 4×8-foot sheet of hardboard, I can get about 40 8×10-inch panels for a total cost of less than $30! Sometimes the cuts are not precise, so that is really the only drawback. When I get these hardboard panels home, I sand the glossy coating off and then prime them with 2 or 3 layers of acrylic gesso. If I want to use an oil primer, I first apply a sizing like rabbit-skin glue to prevent the oil primer from absorbing into the wood.

PAINT APPLICATION

Brushes

Brushes are the most common utensil used to apply oil paint. For plein air painting, I suggest using no more than 3 brushes. Usually, I am so engrossed in the painting process that I simply forget to ever switch out my brush, so I often use just one. But having just a few brushes and varying their size and bristle type will enable you to get some different brush strokes while not overwhelming your decision-making. Plus, the fewer brushes you use, the fewer you need to clean!

Have at least one brush that is large in relation to your painting surface so you can get easy coverage during the block-in stage. Then have maybe one smaller bristle (hog bristle or a synthetic hog bristle) brush and one brush with softer bristles (sable or synthetic brush like taklon). Softer bristles make it easier to apply additional paint over previous layers of paint that are becoming a bit thicker.

Palette Knife

I always have a palette knife with me, but sometimes a knife is the only tool I use to both mix and apply paint. A palette knife is a 3-in-1 tool: mixing, painting, and cleaning. Painting with a palette knife is a great way to get an impressionist look to your paintings as it is a blunt instrument compared to a brush. I also enjoy the quick and easy clean-up—I use the knife to scrape excess paint left over on my palette, and then I can just wipe the knife clean with a paper towel. There is no need for brush cleaning when you paint with just a palette knife.

Shaper Tool

This is a completely optional, but versatile tool for oil and acrylic painters. It is an inexpensive silicone tool with a variety of shaped tips (often sold in a variety pack). They are often used for clay, but if you search for "silicone shaper tool" online, you will find what you're looking for. You can use a shaper tool to carve out thin lines (like power lines and thin twigs), and add texture (think of grass or texture in the trunk of a tree). I mainly use my shaper tool to carve my signature into a bottom corner of my completed (still wet) plein air paintings. Since I pre-tone my panels, carving through the wet paint will reveal the color of my toned panel, which can add a nice pop of color where I place my signature or other small accents on the painting.

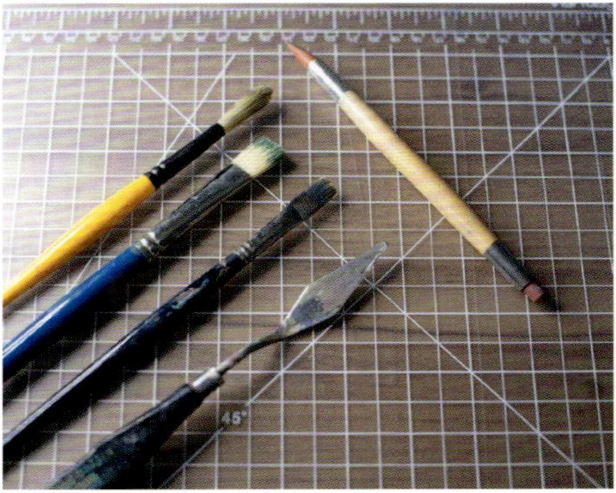

Natural and synthetic hog bristle brushes, a synthetic soft-bristle brush, palette knife, and shaper tool.

TRANSPORTING WET PAINTINGS

It is certainly enough to complete one painting during a plein air session. Whether you're painting for 15 minutes or 4 hours, you get to choose how to spend that time. If you want to complete more than one painting in oil during a single session, you'll need to think about how to safely and cleanly transport any wet painting that can't remain attached to your easel, pochade, or palette.

One option is to purchase a wet panel carrier. To me, these seem to always be a bit more expensive than I'd like, but they look like a great ready-made option. Usually, they require you to use panels within a certain range of sizes, or they might accommodate just one size.

I tend to paint small, so it's easy for me to fit multiple paintings into a cardboard box that is only about an inch thick. I get these boxes from work, and they actually have two levels. I am able to fit four paintings that are 5×7-inches, with a little space between each painting. I roll up a little masking tape to adhere the back of the painting to the cardboard, so my paintings do not shuffle around. Look around you and you may find something surprisingly simple that will serve as protection for wet paintings in transit.

If you have no other option, just be sure that when you get to your vehicle you have an old towel to set your painting on—

preferably on a level surface away from other objects that can fall onto your painting while you're driving.

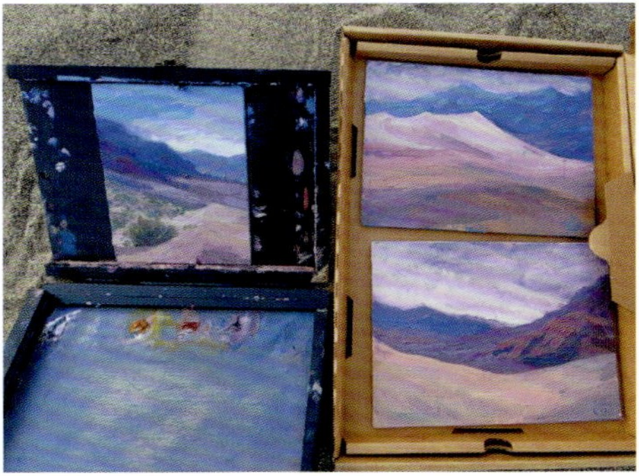

I can store one wet panel in my handheld pochade. The other paintings from the same session are secured with tape inside a slim box.

A Few More Suggestions for Oil Painting Supplies

- Paper towels (I like the blue shop towels best)
- Bags for waste containment and disposal
- Latex gloves (optional). I just don't like getting paint on my hands (even though I'm using non-toxic paint) because it will inevitably end up somewhere else it shouldn't. Plus, they keep my hands warm on cooler days.
- Apron to protect clothing. Bonus if it has pockets!

05 WATERCOLOR & GOUACHE PLEIN AIR MATERIALS

ESSENTIAL WATERCOLOR/GOUACHE PAINTING SETUP

- Painting support of choice (easel, pochade, or a hard-cover sketchbook)
- Paper or board
- Palette of 4 or 5 colors (pans or tubes of paint)
- 1 brush (a maximum of 3) and optional mark-making tools
- Mixed-media items, if desired
- Paper towels, wash cloth, or sponge
- A container for water (water reservoir brush, cup, spray bottle)
- Bag for waste
- Comfort items like beverages, snacks, apron, gloves, hat, etc.

EASEL? POCHADE? SKETCHBOOK? BOARD?

With watercolor painting, you typically want to have a more horizontal angle on which to place your paper as compared to the more vertical angle of oil and acrylic painting. Watercolor runs when very diluted and, while this is desirable to a degree, you probably do not want your color running all the way down and off your paper every time you place it. Many easels and pochade boxes have adjustable angles that will accommodate a gentler slope for watercolor painting. A completely level surface may result in pooling on your paper. This is not the worst outcome since we tend to love the unique "imperfections" of the watercolor character, but just something to be aware of.

Like any other kind of painting, you needn't invest in an expensive easel or pochade to begin watercolor painting. If you have a rigid board, you can use painters' tape or just clips to attach your watercolor paper and simply hold this in your lap while sitting down. If you do this, have a way to protect your clothes from water that may run toward you as many pigments will permanently stain fabric.

A nice feature of watercolor is that it dries quickly. It is very likely that you will have a dry or nearly dry painting at the end of your painting session. This feature makes it much easier to do your plein air paintings in a sketchbook with water media.

At the end of a session, if your painting is dry you can simply close the sketchbook or carry it open back to your home or vehicle. Being fast-dry media, painters who use watercolor or gouache do not need to plan out a way to transport and store paintings that will remain wet for days or weeks.

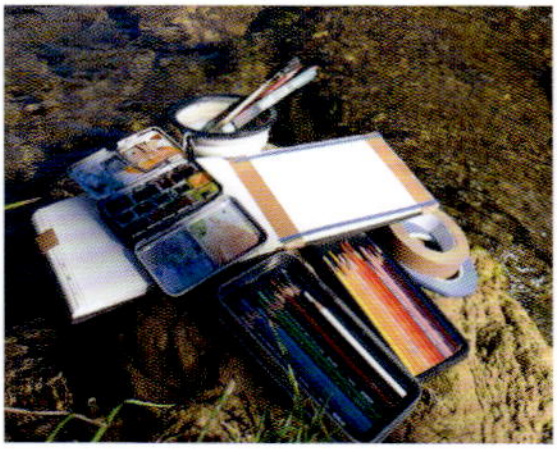

Watercolor materials kit. A magnet holds my metal palette to this sketchbook.

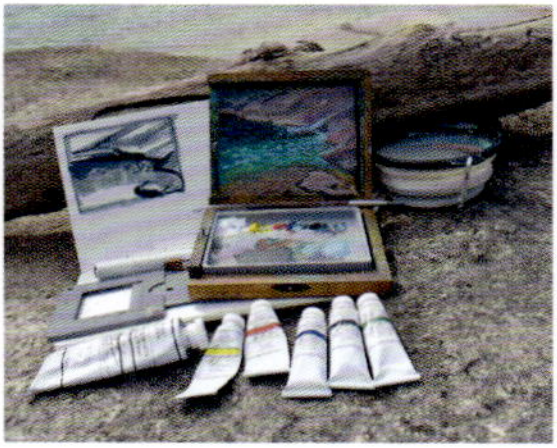

Gouache materials kit. I use my handheld pochade with a 3-D printed insert so I'm not mixing gouache on the same surface where I mix oil paints.

LIMITED PAINT PALETTE

Much of what I wrote about the benefits of using a limited color palette with oil paintings applies to watercolor and gouache as well. However, whereas oil and acrylic painters need to carry at least small tubes of paint with them, watercolor and gouache artists are able to squeeze small amounts of paint into pans (or to purchase already filled pans) that do not take up much space and last for a really long time. This makes it easy to carry around a palette full of dozens of colors in watercolor and gouache.

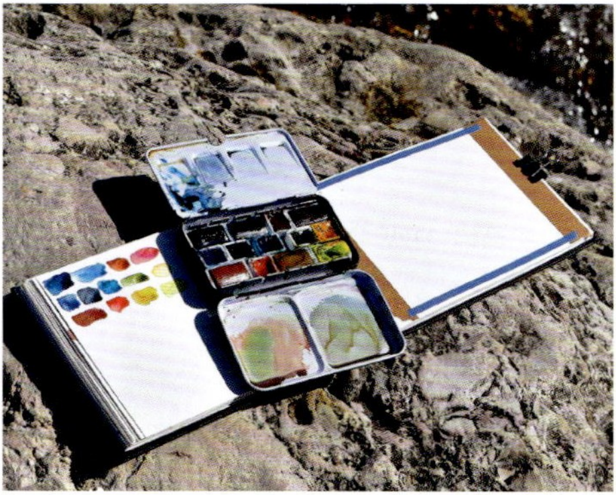

You can see here that I swatched my watercolor palette on the left side of the sketchbook spread. This helps me to choose just a few colors to use, rather than using my colors haphazardly.

The challenge here then is that you may find that you have access to an unmanageable number of colors right at your fingertips. If this is the case, I recommend pre-planning a maximum of five specific colors you will use in a given painting session. I usually do some swatches on scratch paper to choose which colors I'll use and to experiment with how they mix and interact with each other. While I'm painting, I have the locations of those colors mapped out in my mind so I know where to dip my brush. Watercolors in particular can look much darker in their concentrated pan form than they look when diluted with water. So doing some color swatching or a quick color wheel will help you to visualize what some of those darker-appearing colors actually look like on paper.

PANS VS. TUBES

Watercolor and gouache paints both come in either tube or pan form (though it's much less common for gouache to come in pans). Some artists prefer to dispense their paint just before using it, while others prefer to use paint that has settled and dried. Paint squeezed from a tube just before painting will be very malleable and rich. It can border on being too rich (or too concentrated) and difficult to get more diluted mixes for light washes. Paints allowed to dry and settle can have the opposite problem—it can be more difficult to get mixes that are very rich or dark.

With gouache, most people prefer to use it squeezed fresh from the tube. Usually, I'll do a combination. I will use gouache dried in pans for the first layer or two, and then I'll squeeze fresh paint from tubes as needed in the final layer where I need more rich color and opaque coverage. With gouache, it is especially difficult to layer light colors and highlights over previous layers unless you use a white that is still fresh.

I am one who uses watercolor in dried pans almost exclusively. I purchase watercolors mainly in tubes, squeeze them into my own pans (they can be purchased in bulk very cheap), and then I allow them to dry for several days or a week. I like to mix and match different colors in my palette, and these individual pans makes that very easy as they just snap in and out of a metal palette.

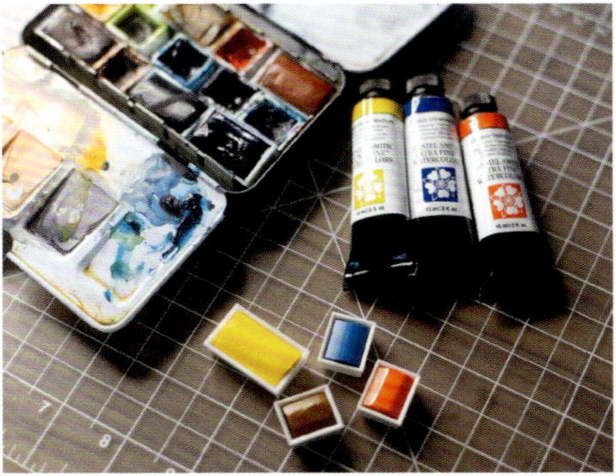

Pans that I poured myself from tubes, compared with pans filled by a paint manufacturer.

Pre-Filled Pans

Many paint manufacturers sell pre-filled pans in addition to tubes. I haven't done the math to know which is the better option from an economic standpoint, but they are probably pretty close. The pre-filled pans often seem to be more concentrated than the watercolor in tube form. If I compare a pan that I filled myself from a tube with a pre-filled pan, it seems like the pre-filled pan lasts longer. This is just a hunch on my part. Pre-filled pans are nice because they are very uniform. I sometimes buy these and use them to pop in and out of my metal palette.

QUALITY AND FEATURES

As stated earlier in this guide, I do not have a brand that I stick to exclusively. Different brands offer unique pigments with varying qualities that are more or less desirable. I find Winsor & Newton watercolors to be very rich and affordable. Daniel Smith watercolors can offer some really beautiful granulating pigments and a huge selection of colors. Gouache made by M. Graham contains honey, which makes it stay malleable, while Winsor & Newton gouache dries more brittle and is prone to cracking, but it's great for fresh use. There are too many nuances and factors to consider, so I recommend focusing on purchasing just a few basic colors of the highest quality you can afford. A great starting point is a set of three primary colors sold by Daniel Smith.

WHITE GOUACHE

Obviously, you will use white gouache when painting with gouache, but artists have varying opinions about using white gouache with watercolor paintings. Some refer to white gouache as "opaque watercolor," but it is in fact not watercolor. Those who take pride in painting purely with watercolor (retaining the white of their paper for the lighter values and highlights in their paintings) do not use white gouache. But many artists do use white gouache to add highlights on top of their watercolor paintings. When painting en plein air, it can be difficult to retain specific whites because we are working very quickly. Small, delicate highlights—even when marked off during the drawing phase—can get lost in a wash or inadvertently covered. Unless you strive to be a watercolorist who works strictly with watercolor, go ahead and keep a tube of white gouache handy. It might make an important difference to your own satisfaction to be able to add some white back into your piece.

MIXED MEDIA

Both watercolor and gouache are particularly well-suited for mixed media. In fact, using watercolor and gouache together is a form of mixed media. You can make any of your watercolors more opaque by adding a little gouache to them (most commonly, you might add white to your transparent watercolors to create a more opaque color application).

I also like to use colored pencil and ink with both watercolor and gouache paintings. Colored pencil can add some texture and structure to a watercolor painting that is a bit wild or chaotic. You might also notice that a lot of urban sketchers (plein air painting in an urban setting) use loose washes of watercolor along with ink lines and hatching. You might consider experimenting with pastels, charcoal, or just about anything you can think of to mix with your watercolor or gouache. You can even apply an oil-based medium like oil pastels on top of water-based media (you just can't apply a water-based media over an oil-based media).

PALETTE CHOICES

Metal

Metal palettes are very versatile, and they don't have to be expensive. You should be able to find one for $20 or less that will hold several pans of paint, and they usually fold out so you have one or two mixing areas. The only drawback I encounter is that the water can cause the metal to rust a bit, so it's advisable to dry it off with a paper towel when you're done for the day.

I really like that you can snap pans of watercolor or gouache in and out of a metal palette very easily. This enables me to switch up my colors without having to wait to use up a color so that I can refill that space with a different color. It takes me a really long time to use up an entire pan of watercolor or gouache because I switch up my colors frequently.

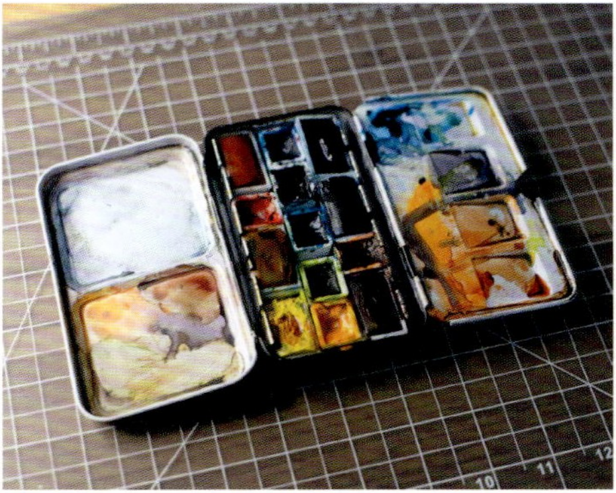

Another reason I love metal palettes is that they are magnetic. I have some strong magnets that I can use to attach my metal palette to either a sketchbook or to the board I have my paper clipped to. This places my palette in close proximity to my painting and eliminates the need for me to set it on a different surface or to hold it in my non-dominant hand.

Plastic

Plastic palettes are lightweight and usually contain many wells that can be filled with watercolor or gouache from tubes. I really like the large mixing areas in plastic palettes. Other palettes tend to have smaller and fewer compartments dedicated to mixing and I like to have several separate mixes going. What I don't like as much about my plastic palette is that I'm kind of stuck with whatever colors I've filled the wells with until they are used up, and it takes a really long time for me to use them up. It would be a good idea just to fill these wells partially, but I almost always feel so passionately devoted to a color in the moment that I fill the well up completely and then it lasts for a year or more. The other reason I don't use my plastic palette as much as my metal palette is because it is not magnetic. I could glue a magnet to it, but I just pick up my metal palette when I want this feature, which I usually do.

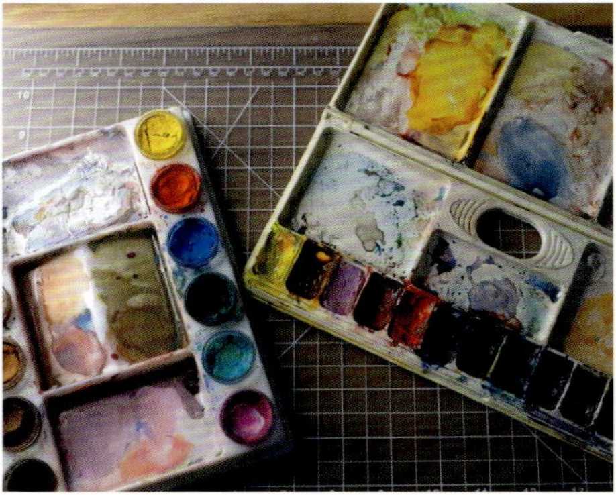

Dried gouache (left) and watercolor (right) in plastic palettes.

Ceramic

Ceramic is my preferred mixing surface for watercolor and gouache when I'm in my studio. However, being that it is heavy and breakable, it is not well-suited to plein air painting. Some artists prefer it so much that they bring their ceramic palettes out into the field.

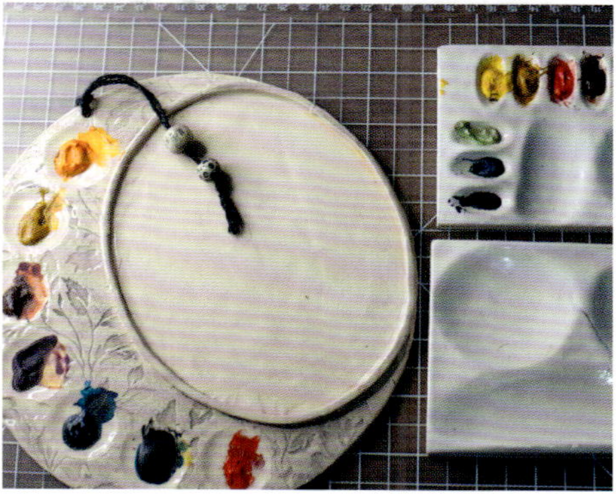

These ceramic palettes are too heavy and fragile for painting in the field, but it's a lovely surface for watercolor in the studio. Both of these palettes were custom made by ceramic artists on Etsy.

BRUSHES AND OTHER MARK-MAKING UTENSILS

Water Reservoir Brushes

These brushes are really great for plein air painting with watercolor or gouache. I will often begin my painting session by filling up one of these brushes, leaving the brush portion off, and squeezing water from the brush onto my paints to begin activating them. I don't usually carry a spray bottle with me, and I find that squeezing water from my brush reservoir is easier to control than a spray anyway. The intended function of a water reservoir brush is to squeeze it through the bristles to add water to the paint that is on the bristles. With practice, you can become adept at controlling this flow throughout the painting process. It can eliminate the need to have a cup of water next to you, although I usually have one anyway and end up using my reservoir brush just like a regular brush.

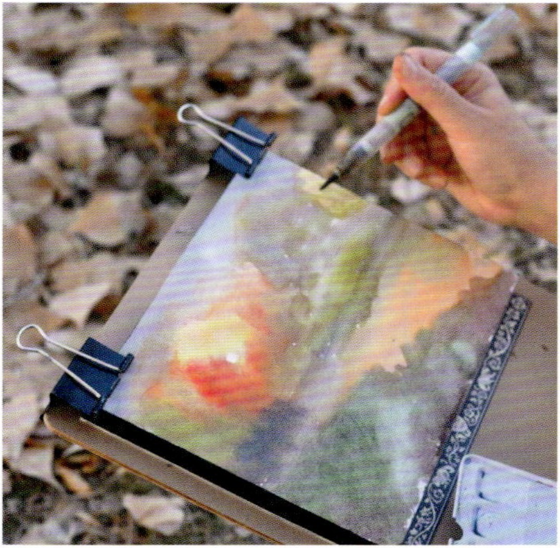

Using a brush with a water reservoir is a great option for plein air painting in watercolor or gouache.

Mop Brushes

Mop brushes can be made of natural fibers like squirrel, or they can be synthetic. Either way, they are meant to soak up a lot of water and are great for applying washes. However, you can also use them beyond washes as the bristles, not entirely saturated with water, can sharpen to a fine point and be used to apply darker values with less concentrated paint, and to make thin marks. I use mop brushes a lot with watercolor, but not much with gouache. Sometimes I'll use a hake brush for large washes.

Taklon and Other Synthetic Brushes

I really like taklon brushes with gouache paint. The bristles are soft, but firmer than the bristles of a mop brush. With gouache, I use thicker paint and not as many washes, so it's nice to have these firm bristles to push the paint around. These brushes are useful with watercolor to apply your paint more thickly in the final layer. They are also good for dry brush techniques since the bristles do not hold a lot of water.

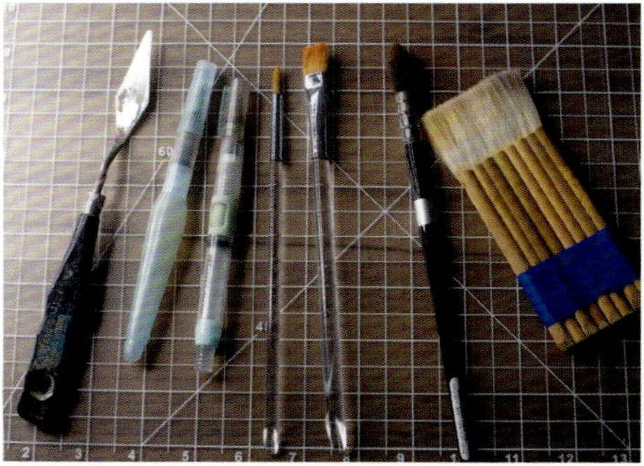

Various tools for watercolor and gouache painting: A palette knife for scraping, two water reservoir brushes, two taklon brushes, squirrel mop brush, hake brush.

Scraper for Textures and Lines

You might be surprised to see a palette knife sometimes in my watercolor kit. Much like how I use a shaper tool in oil painting to carve into and remove paint, I use a palette knife in my watercolor and gouache paintings to scrape away paint that hasn't completely dried yet. This is a great way to add texture or to scrape out thin lines in branches or wire fences. If you do not have a palette knife, an old card (like a hotel key card or gift card) will do the trick. You can even cut your card in such a way to create a sharper point. You could use this to add little glints of reflection to water, to add a highlight back into an area that got covered with paint, or even to scratch your signature into your painting.

Pencil/Colored Pencil

I already mentioned using mixed media (like colored pencil) with your watercolor or gouache paintings, but you can use these to a more limited and subtle extent just to add a little structure to your painting. A few strategically placed lines with a pencil or colored pencil can make a painting that feels a bit chaotic suddenly make sense.

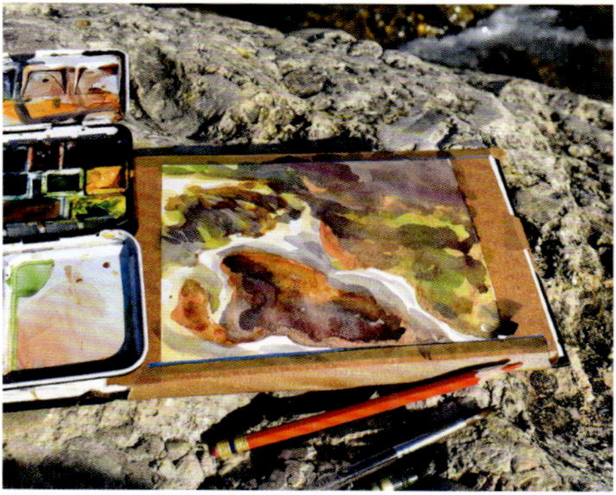

I often like to use a red or orange colored pencil to do the drawing under my watercolor paintings. If you look closely, you can see these lines. I think it adds character to watercolor to allow the drawing to show through.

PAPER/SUBSTRATES FOR WATERCOLOR AND GOUACHE

Blocks vs. Sheets vs. Boards

The two most common formats for papers is a rigid support with tape or clips to attach loose sheets, or a "block" of paper that is glued together and forms a rigid support in itself. Loose sheets are nice because you can cut the paper down to smaller sheets if you'd like. It's also easier to have multiple paintings going simultaneously if you have sheets attached to a couple of boards. I like to work on two watercolor paintings simultaneously because if I'm waiting for one painting to dry so I can do some wet-on-dry applications, I can entertain myself with another painting on the side that is maybe more experimental. To do this with blocks means I need to have more than one block. And since they contain a lot of paper, they are each pretty expensive. So, when I paint with a block, I'm more likely to be working on only one painting. Although, I suppose I could have my sketchbook nearby.

The advantage of a block is that you don't need to spend any time fixing it to a rigid support. These days, I just use bulldog clips to do this so it doesn't really take up much time. But I used to use painters' tape and it would frustrate me if my tape didn't line up perfectly with the edge of the paper. Some artists "stretch" their watercolor paper by pre-soaking it and then attaching it to a rigid support, but I've never done this. Blocks of paper do not require stretching and they are less prone to buckling, pooling, and otherwise warping. An excessive amount of water can still cause these problems with watercolor blocks, but it is less common. One of my favorite surfaces on which to paint with gouache (and watercolor works well, too) is illustration board. This acid-free, artist grade substrate is essentially a nice cardboard that is made for artists and illustrators. Crescent is the brand I use. I buy it in packs of large sheets and then I use a utility knife to cut it down to the small sizes I like.

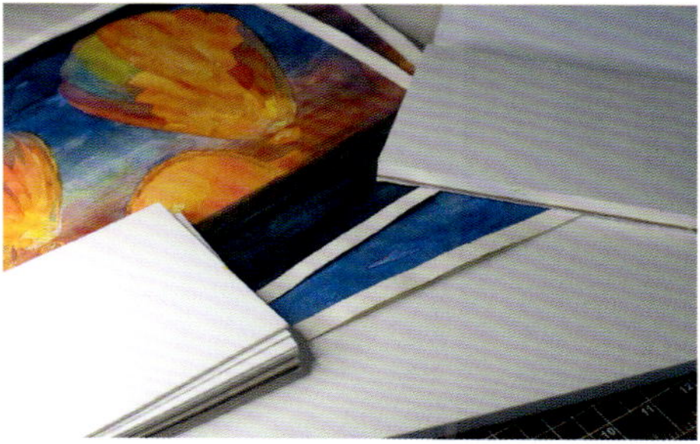

Watercolor paper in block and sheet form, multiple sizes. On the larger sheets that are painted, you'll see a white border where I taped the paper to a rigid backing. I do not apply tape to block paper, so those paintings will not have this border.

Sketchbook

With either watercolor or gouache, using a sketchbook is very handy and compact. You don't really need special paper, just make sure it is at least 100-pound weight and somewhat absorbent. As mentioned previously, I really like to use my metal palette with a magnet to attach it to my sketchbook on the opposite side of the spread that I'm painting on. I can be standing or sitting with my sketchbook and palette in my non-dominant hand, and a with water reservoir brush in the other hand, I'm a completely self-contained art-making unit.

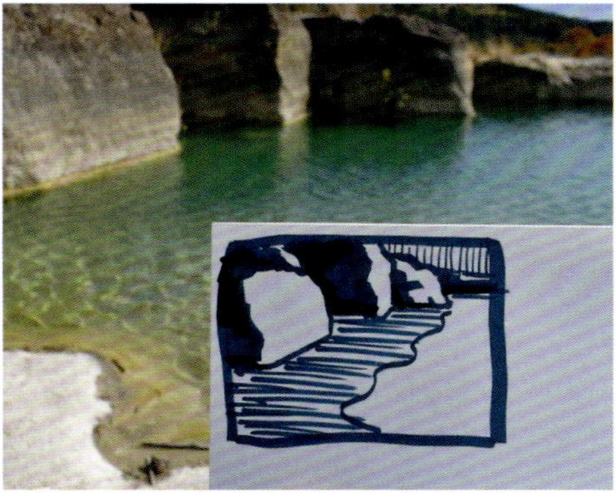

WATER CONTAINER AND SPRAY BOTTLE

If you don't have a water reservoir brush, you'll need a separate container for water. Sometimes I use a collapsible silicone bowl, or I will fill an old glass jar with a lid with water to take with me. If I'm painting near a body of water, I'll almost always get my water on location from that source. I think that's a neat way to incorporate nature into my painting, though it is evident to nobody but me. Personally, I rarely use a spray bottle to reactivate my watercolor or gouache, but for many artists this is an essential tool. I just squeeze water from my water reservoir brush, or I saturate my mop brush and squeeze water from that onto my dry paints.

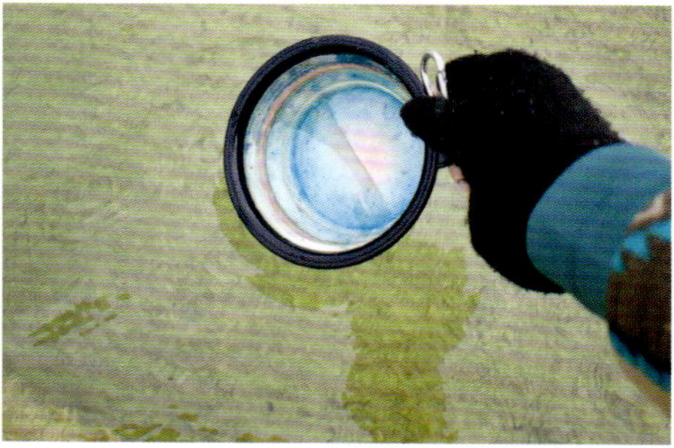

I really love when I can use water from the location where I'm painting. I feel like it is a subtle way to bring nature into my art.

Paper Towels, Wash Cloth, Sponge

You'll want a way to blot off excess water from your brush, or to wipe off pigment. You can use paper towels, but unlike oil and acrylic paint, watercolor and gouache won't gunk up your towel. Therefore, I'll just use an old washcloth. The pigment will permanently stain it, but you can just rinse it off and reuse it indefinitely. You may also find it useful to have a sponge on which you can blot your brush, and you can also use it to apply water or texture to your painting.

06 PAINTING AND SKETCHING PROCESSES

Here are some examples of paintings using different mediums.

OIL PAINTING (1)

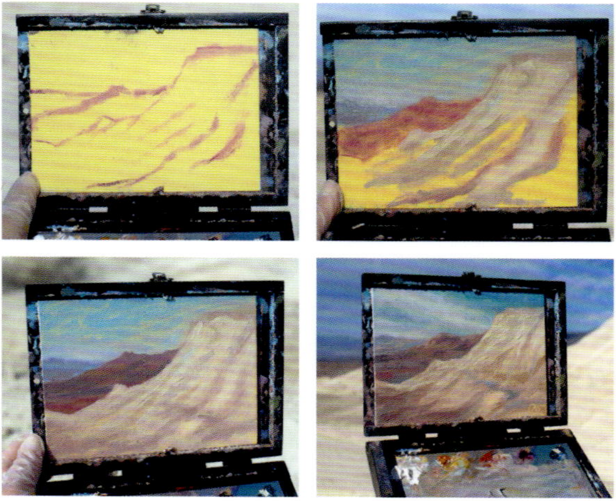

OIL PAINTING (2)

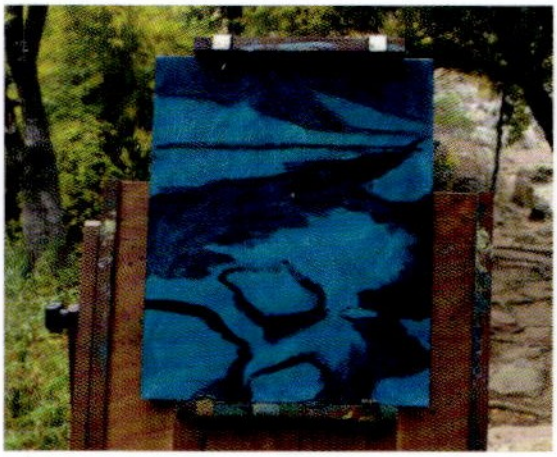

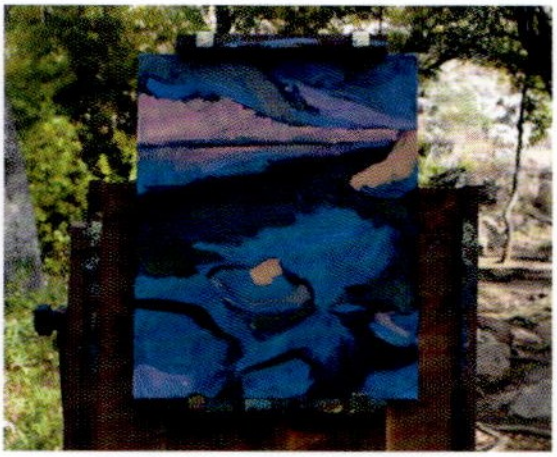

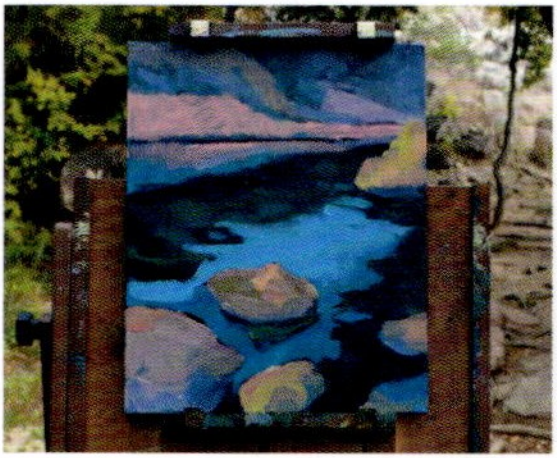

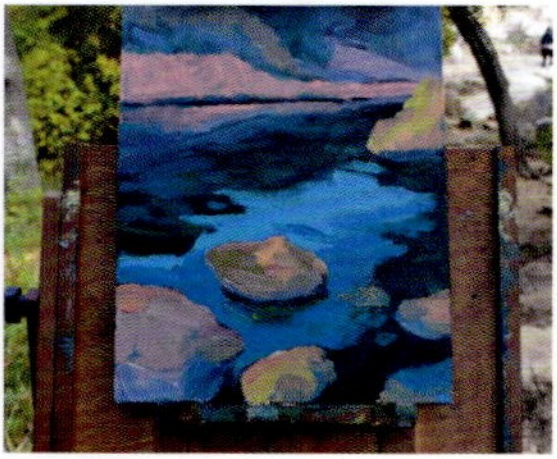

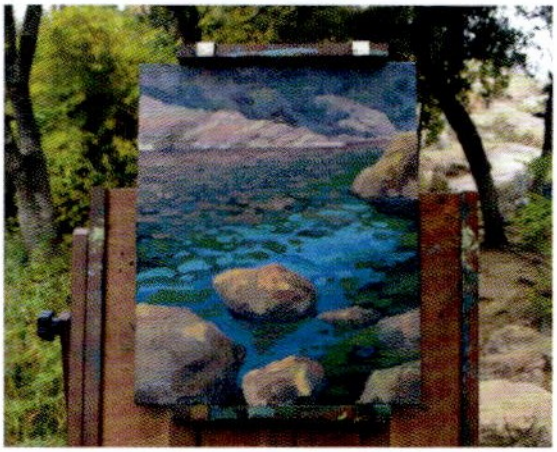

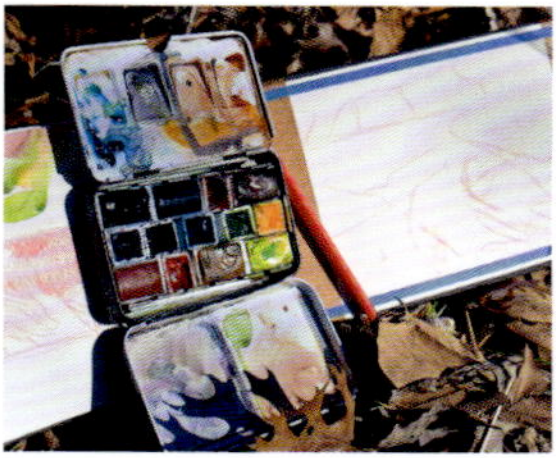

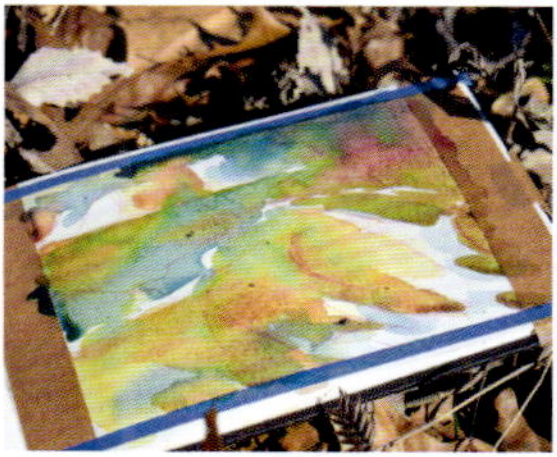

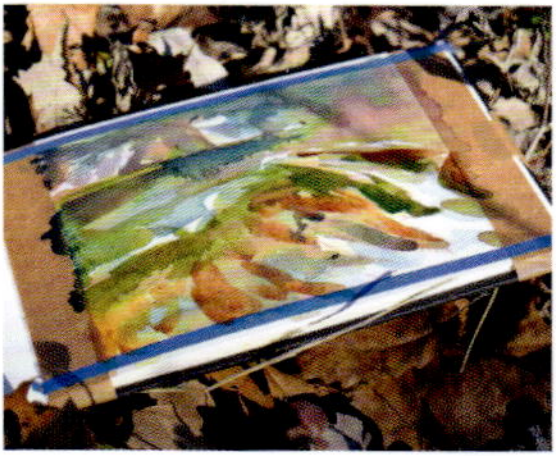

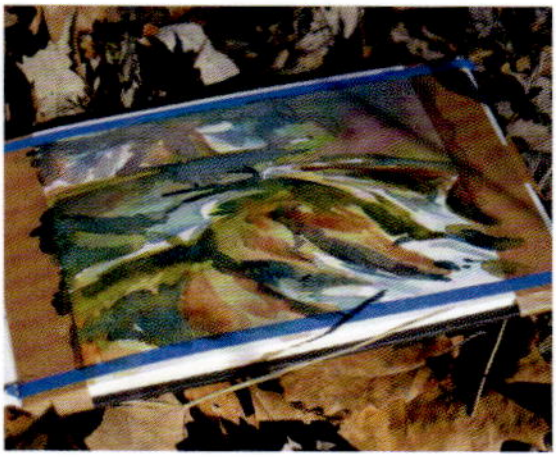

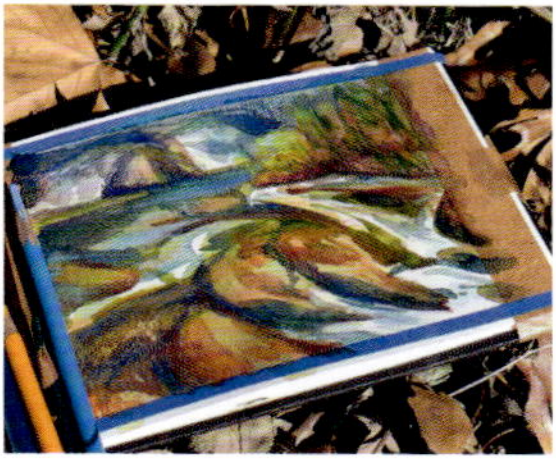

GOUACHE PAINTING

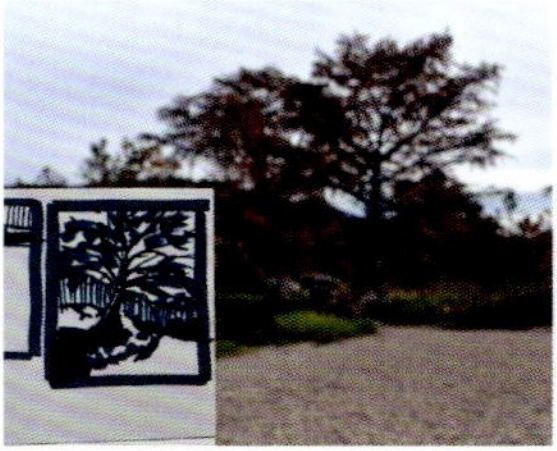
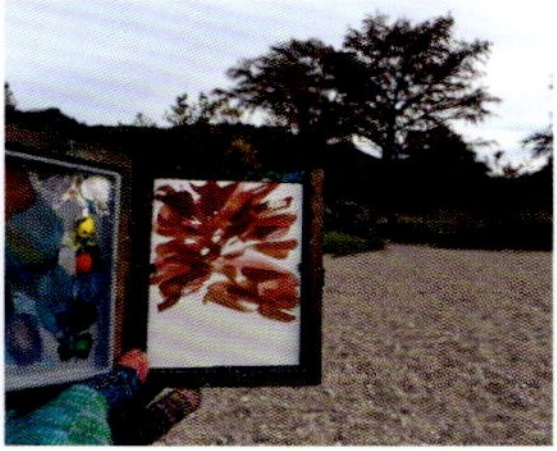
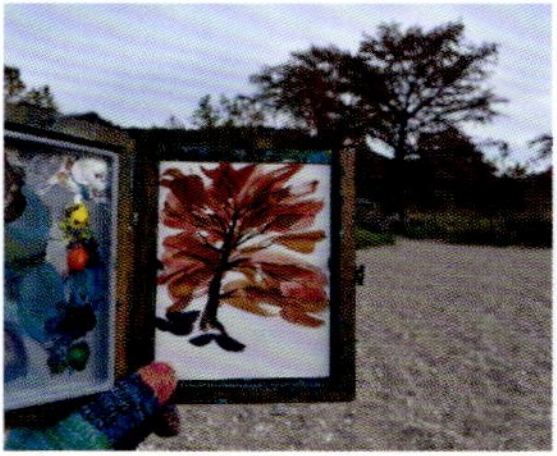
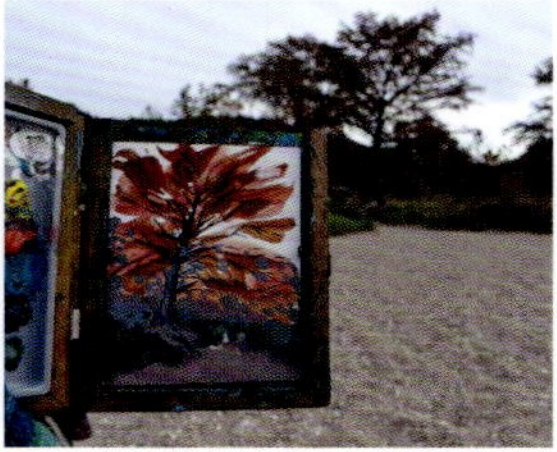
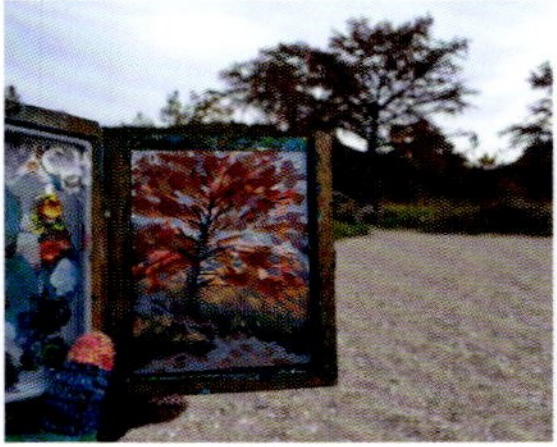
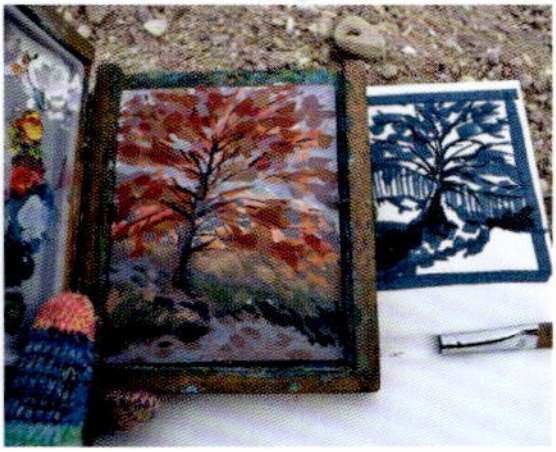

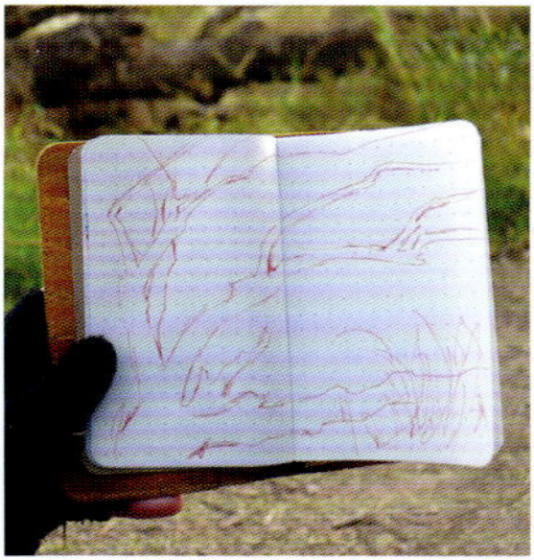

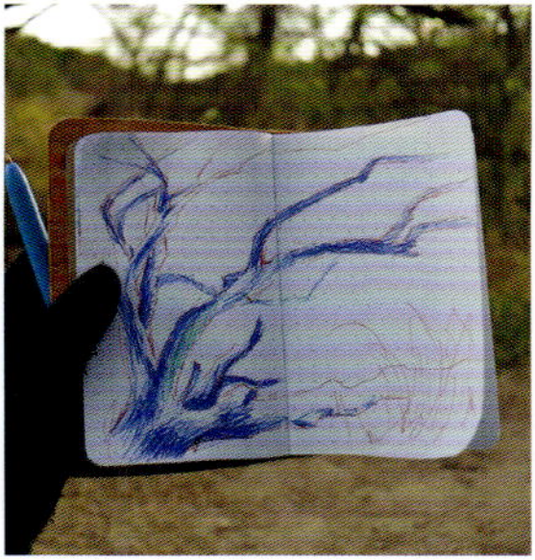

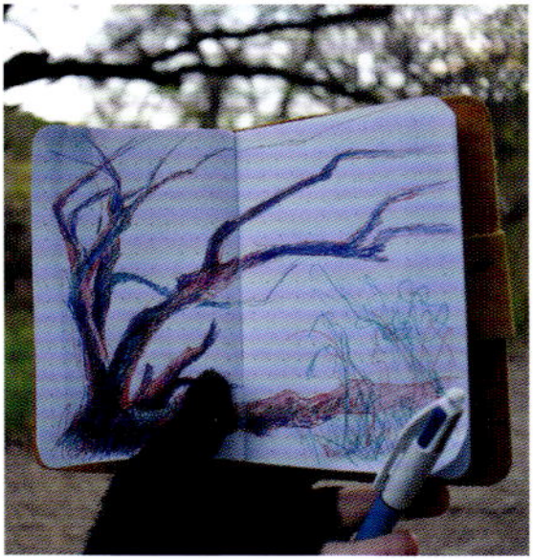

A FEW EXAMPLES OF MY PLEIN AIR WORK

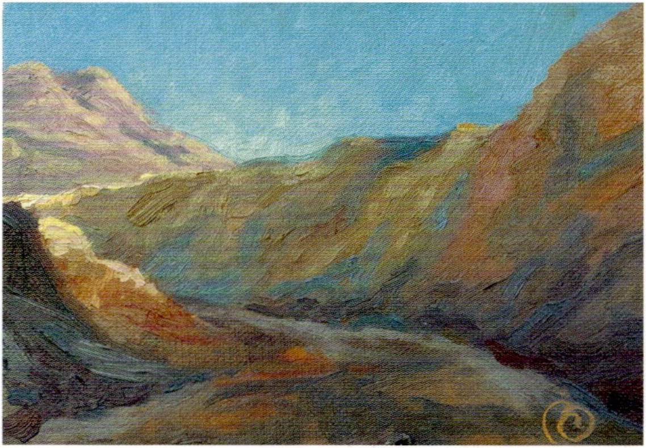

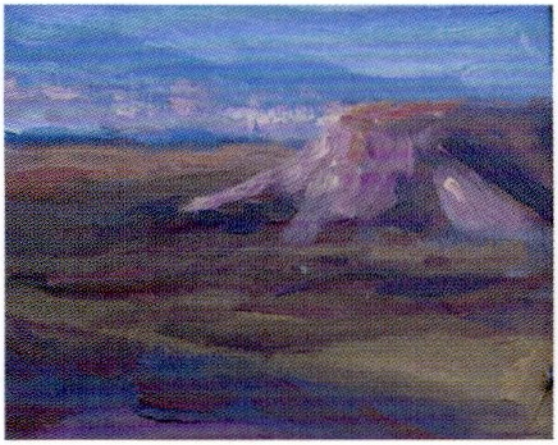

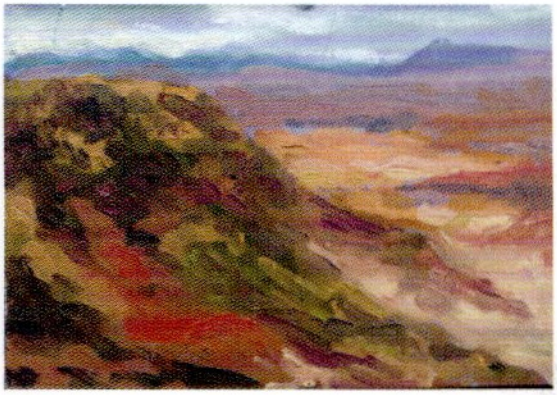